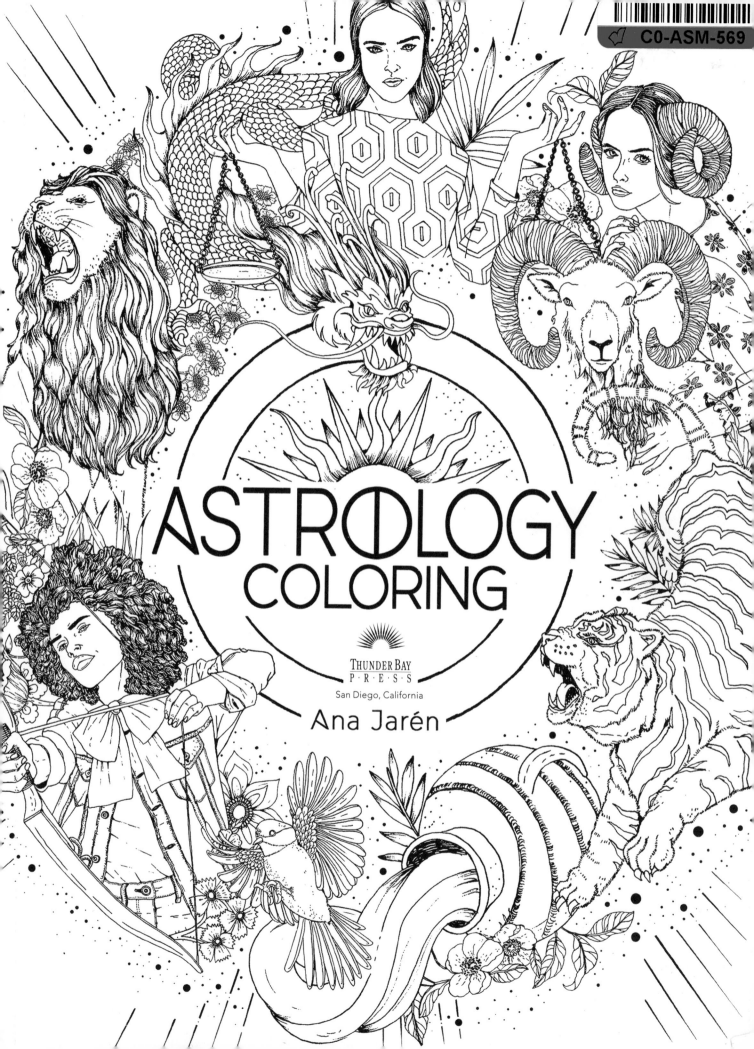

ASTROLOGY COLORING

THUNDER BAY
P·R·E·S·S
San Diego, California

Ana Jarén

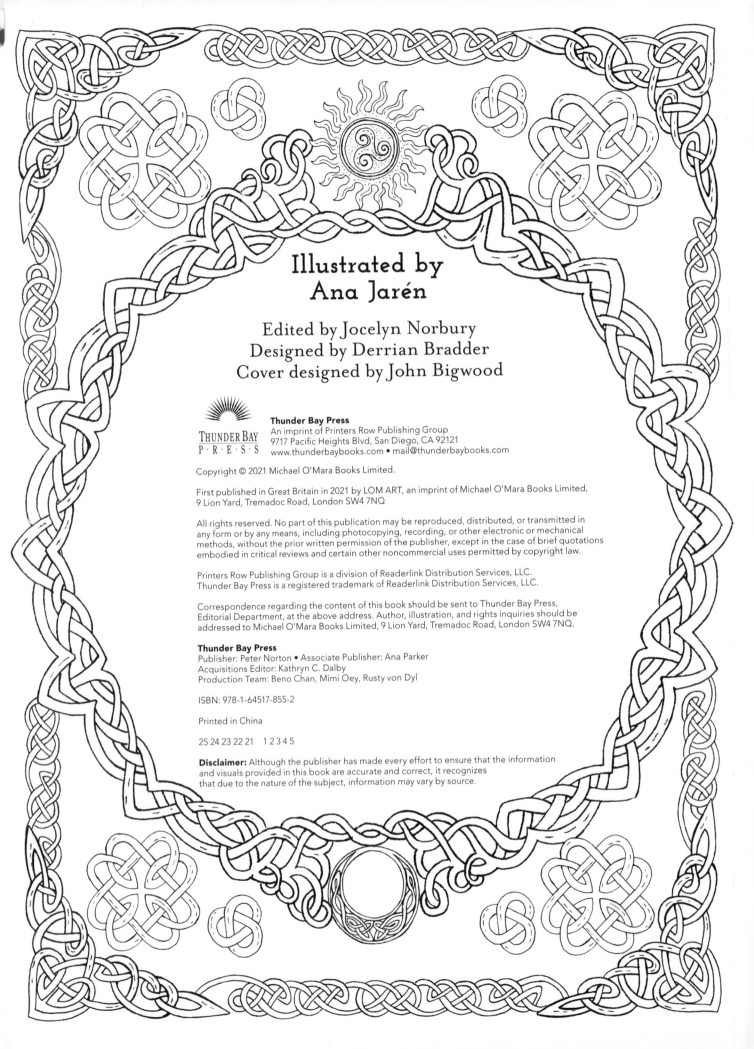

Illustrated by
Ana Jarén

Edited by Jocelyn Norbury
Designed by Derrian Bradder
Cover designed by John Bigwood

Thunder Bay Press
An imprint of Printers Row Publishing Group
9717 Pacific Heights Blvd, San Diego, CA 92121
www.thunderbaybooks.com • mail@thunderbaybooks.com

Copyright © 2021 Michael O'Mara Books Limited.

First published in Great Britain in 2021 by LOM ART, an imprint of Michael O'Mara Books Limited,
9 Lion Yard, Tremadoc Road, London SW4 7NQ

Printers Row Publishing Group is a division of Readerlink Distribution Services, LLC.
Thunder Bay Press is a registered trademark of Readerlink Distribution Services, LLC.

Correspondence regarding the content of this book should be sent to Thunder Bay Press,
Editorial Department, at the above address. Author, illustration, and rights inquiries should be
addressed to Michael O'Mara Books Limited, 9 Lion Yard, Tremadoc Road, London SW4 7NQ.

Thunder Bay Press
Publisher: Peter Norton • Associate Publisher: Ana Parker
Acquisitions Editor: Kathryn C. Dalby
Production Team: Beno Chan, Mimi Oey, Rusty von Dyl

ISBN: 978-1-64517-855-2

Printed in China

25 24 23 22 21   1 2 3 4 5

Disclaimer: Although the publisher has made every effort to ensure that the information
and visuals provided in this book are accurate and correct, it recognizes
that due to the nature of the subject, information may vary by source.

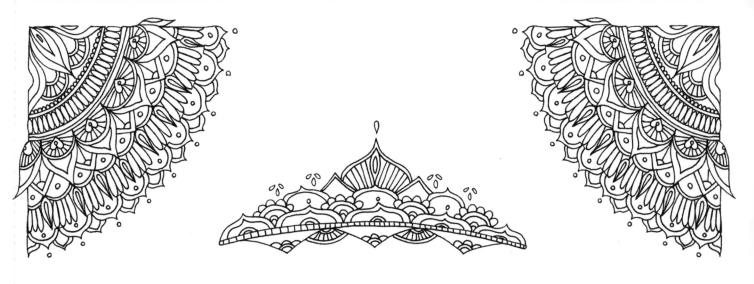

Introduction

For over 2,000 years, the night sky and the celestial bodies that populate it have fascinated civilizations around the world. From the ancient Greeks and Egyptians to the Druids and Mayans, people have used astrology to help understand themselves and their place in the universe. The study of the stars has provided inspiration for myths and legends passed down through generations.

Embark on a journey of discovery as you color your way around the cosmos. Explore the history of zodiac systems from around the world and discover more about the fascinating elements of the Greek and Chinese systems.

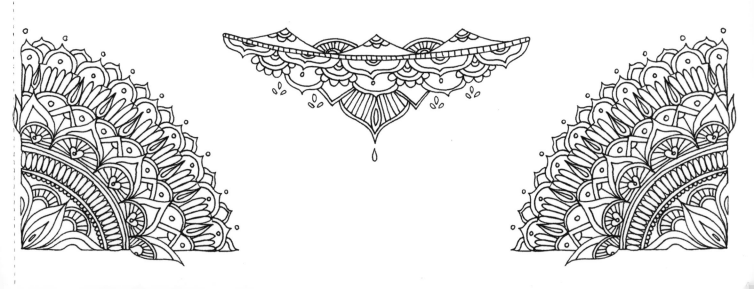

Constellations

Of the eighty-eight constellations that glitter in the night sky, only twelve are linked to signs of the Greek zodiac. These twelve are aligned so that the Sun appears to travel through them during the year.

But what is a constellation? Stars in the galaxy are scattered across a vast, three-dimensional space. When viewed from Earth, they appear as two-dimensional shapes. These shapes are associated with pictures that are linked to magical myths and legends.

The Greek Zodiac

One of the most ancient and well-known
zodiac systems, the Greek zodiac is based
around twelve groups of stars, or constellations.

The twelve constellations are Aries, Taurus, Gemini, Cancer,
Leo, Virgo, Libra, Scorpio, Sagittarius, Capricorn, Aquarius,
and Pisces. An individual's sign can be determined by the date
of their birth. Each sign has its own symbol and association
with a Greek god or goddess, whose special characteristics
inform the qualities associated with that sign.

Aries the Ram

Aries, the first sign of the Greek zodiac, is based on the legend of a flying ram with a magnificent golden fleece who rescued a child from a horrible death.

People born under this sign of the fire element are blessed with a confident and heroic spirit. Their determination and headstrong nature are indicated by the ram's powerful horns.

Taurus the Bull

Noble and steadfast, Taurus is one of the most stable and dependable signs of the Greek zodiac. However, there is more to this strong and silent earth sign than meets the eye. Taureans possess an ethereal energy that is associated with spiritual awakening as well as beauty and sensuality.

Gemini the Twins

Greek legend has it that strong, powerful, and determined twins Castor and Pollux possess power over the wind and waves to keep sailors safe from shipwreck.

Accordingly, people born under this sign of the air element place great importance on companionship. With their fun-loving and inquisitive nature, Geminis are attractive to others and find it easy to form new relationships.

Cancer the Crab

With a hard outer shell protecting its hidden
vulnerability, the cautious crab is said to use its
claws to cling to the comfortable and familiar in
Greek astrology.

Nurturing and sensitive, people born under
this water sign are governed by emotion. They
seek security first and foremost, and place
great value on home comforts.

Leo the Lion

Regal and charismatic, the lion radiates power
and is often associated with leadership. A true
fire sign, Leos are driven by creativity and are
on a never-ending quest for self-discovery.

Always noble, though sometimes arrogant,
people of this sign use their power
to protect and honor.

Virgo the Virgin

The ancient Greeks associated the constellation of Virgo
with Demeter, the goddess of agriculture. The earth
sign that ushers summer into fall, Virgo's power
lies in the ability to prepare and plan for change.

The expression "You reap what you sow" takes on particular
resonance for people born under this sign, as their methodical
and hard-working nature helps them achieve their goals.

Libra the Scales

Balance is at the heart of this air sign—the only
sign of the Greek zodiac with an inanimate
object as its symbol. In Greek mythology, Libra
is linked to the goddess of justice, Themis, who
upholds the balance of the seasons and lives
in perfect harmony with nature.

Librans excel at taking differing views
into consideration and believe that
seeking what is best for others can be
the route to a harmonious life for all.

Scorpio the Scorpion

The only water sign that is not depicted as an animal
of its element, the Scorpio symbol traditionally comes
with connotations of danger and aggression.

While it is true that people born under this sign
have strong self-protective tendencies, Scorpions are also
known for their selfless instinct to use power for good.

Sagittarius the Archer

Adventurous, athletic, and wild, people born
under the sign of Sagittarius scatter interests
like arrows and often provide something of
a roller-coaster ride in relationships.

A sign of the fire element, Sagittarians
value excitement and adventure
above almost all else.

Capricorn the Sea Goat

The improbable half-fish, half-goat creature from the Greek legend Pricus started life as a water-dweller but made its way to dry land. Thus, Capricorn became an earth sign.

Like the other earth signs, Capricorns are grounded and practical, but also adaptable, with a strong sense of self-discipline that can help them to achieve great things.

Aquarius the Water Bearer

Aquarius represents life and nourishment—the cleansing water washing away the past in preparation for a fresh start.

Like the other air signs, Aquarians look to the future and focus on growth, both spiritually and intellectually. Known for their independent, free-thinking spirit, people of this sign have a vision of equality and individuality for all.

Pisces the Fish

The Pisces fish, which are always depicted
swimming in opposite directions, represent the
ongoing challenge of balancing fantasy and reality.

Compassionate, intuitive, and open-minded,
people born under this water sign have a gentle,
empathetic nature and sometimes need help to
stay grounded in the material realm.

Ophiuchus the Serpent Bearer

Often referred to as the "thirteenth sign" of the Greek zodiac, Ophiuchus is not featured in traditional astrology. Although the Sun does pass in front of this astronomical constellation, it is only due to a shift in the Earth's path over time—this was not the case when the signs were originally designated. If added to the zodiac calendar, Ophiuchus would fall between Scorpio and Sagittarius.

Represented by a figure grasping a snake, Ophiuchus represents courage, bravery, and strength.

The Chinese Zodiac

The Chinese zodiac, known as Sheng Xiao, plays an essential role in Chinese culture and features twelve animal signs: Rat, Ox, Tiger, Rabbit, Dragon, Snake, Horse, Goat, Monkey, Rooster, Dog, and Pig.

Like the Greek zodiac, the Chinese system is based on date and time of birth. Its origins can be traced back more than 2,000 years. The twelve signs, repeating in a twelve-year cycle, are not only used to represent years but are also believed to influence people's personalities, careers, compatibility, and fortunes.

The Great Race

This famous story plays an important part in the history of the Chinese zodiac. Legend has it that the Jade Emperor, one of the most important gods in traditional Chinese religion, organized a race. He invited all of the animals in the world to participate and promised to name a zodiac year after each animal that took part.

The race, which involved crossing a treacherous river, allowed the animals to prove their strength, cunning, or speed. Their finishing position in the race determines their order in the zodiac to this day, and stories relating to the race are used to illustrate the key characteristics of the twelve animal signs.

The Year of the Rat

Wily and wise, the Rat ranks first in the Chinese zodiac. Representing wealth and good fortune, it is considered one of the luckiest signs to be born under.

A sign of great optimism, the Rat symbolizes the dawn of a new day, and the hope and opportunity this brings.

The Year of the Ox

The appeal of the Ox lies not only in its honest
and hard-working nature, but also in its quiet elegance that
can be somewhat at odds with the solidity of its appearance.

Low-key and discreet, people born under this
sign use their strong sense of self-belief
to achieve their goals.

The Year of the Tiger

The powerful, confident, and brave Tiger is known
as the king of the forest in Chinese mythology.

Possessing a quiet energy to carry them through the
toughest situations, people born under this sign
know that anything is possible and that no
obstacle is insurmountable.

The Year of the Rabbit

With lively, twitching ears and large, watchful eyes,
the Rabbit symbolizes vigilance and caution, as well
as good luck in Chinese lore. In ancient times, a rabbit
emblem was used to protect armies going into battle.

To this day, those born under this sign are thought
to be well versed in self-preservation.

The Year of the Dragon

One of the most important and powerful symbols in
Chinese culture, the dragon was once considered so sacred
that its image could only be used in royal settings.

Strong yet gentle, wise, and selfless, this beautiful,
mythical creature represents the importance of balance
in all things—the ultimate embodiment of yin and yang.

The Year of the Snake

Enigmatic with a palpable air of danger, the Snake—which may look intimidating—is blessed with many positive gifts. With its unusual, otherworldly elegance, a charming snake can cast a hypnotic spell.

People of this sign—who are intelligent, if somewhat opportunistic—challenge judgment and are always full of surprises.

The Year of the Horse

Representing stamina, growth, and progression, the Horse is an important symbol of freedom in Chinese culture. According to one Great Race story, the Horse was too frightened to pass through a cemetery on the race route. The delay meant it could only claim seventh place in the final ranking, despite its strength and speed.

Motivated by happiness rather than material gain, people born under this sign pursue all dreams with enthusiasm. No dream is too wild and fantastical or too small and insignificant.

The Year of the Goat

The Goat is a symbol of purity and kindness.
With its protective horns, this noble animal
presents an armored exterior that belies
a gentle, sensitive character within.

Just as goats were traditionally presented as
tokens of luck, so too this sign is considered
one of the luckiest in the Chinese zodiac.

The Year of the Monkey

The magical fruit of the peento peach tree is thought
to guarantee eternal youth. The Monkey's love of
peaches has ensured that it, too, is associated with
longevity and prosperity.

Often smart and logical, people born under
this sign have the ability to turn even negative
experiences into life lessons, thereby snatching
victory from the jaws of defeat.

The Year of the Rooster

Considered tenacious, insightful, and particular, people born under the sign of the Rooster never fail to set high standards for themselves and others.

Associated with early mornings, the Rooster's "seize the day" approach teaches us to grasp opportunity when it presents itself.

The Year of the Dog

The principled hound is noteworthy for its
loyalty and honesty—a genuine best friend.

Protective of those close to them, people born
under this sign have trustworthy characters
and will protect and defend others
even at their own expense.

The Year of the Pig

There is never a dull moment with the energetic and
entertaining people born under this sociable sign.

An infectious enthusiasm and hard-working
nature means that people born in the year
of the Pig will always reach for the stars,
regardless of the odds.

The Cat

Despite playing a part in the Great Race
story, the Cat is not one of the twelve animals
named in the Chinese calendar.

Legend has it that on the day of the
Great Race, the Rat—supposedly a great friend
of the Cat—left it sleeping, forcing it to miss the
race and be denied a place in the ranking.
Furious to have missed this opportunity, cats
can be found chasing rats to this day.

Elements: Earth

Representing strength and stability, earth is the
matter from which everything grows.

The earth element has the power to ground us, and cultivating
our earth energy allows us to find our place in the world. Deep
and solid foundations enable us to move through life with the
knowledge that we are safe and secure.

The earth elements in the Greek zodiac are Taurus, Virgo,
and Capricorn. In the Chinese zodiac, the earth element
governs the Ox, Dragon, Goat, and Dog signs.

Elements: Water

Water can be a powerful, unstoppable torrent or a flowing, gentle, and nurturing life force. As such, it is no surprise that the water element is strongly linked to the world of emotions. Water signs are typically highly sensitive and empathetic and, like a boat thrown off course by stormy seas, their sense of self can be easily rocked by the opinions of others.

The water signs in the Greek zodiac are Cancer, Scorpio, and Pisces. Water is not one of the elements in Chinese astrology.

Elements: Fire

The fire element is concerned with three things:
creation, destruction, and transformation.

The sheer energy of fire can be difficult to contain and
control, but when channeled positively, it can be an
unstoppable force for change. Persistent and strong, fire
is associated with passion as well as aggression.

The fire signs in the Greek zodiac are Aries, Leo, and
Sagittarius. In the Chinese system, the fire element
governs the Snake and Horse signs.

Elements: Air

Though it is invisible, air plays an important role in connecting the other elements. It has strong associations with freedom, literally providing the means to breathe, expand, and grow.

Air signs can be whimsical and often require a grounding influence to prevent them from floating away on a breeze of fancy. The air signs in the Greek zodiac are Gemini, Libra, and Aquarius. Like water, air is not one of the elements in Chinese astrology.

Elements: Wood

Just as wood is known for its warmth and tactile quality, the wood element is the most "human" of the elements in the Chinese zodiac. Associated with growth, expansion, and planning for the future, wood governs the Chinese zodiac signs Tiger, Rabbit, and Dragon.

Elements: Metal

Metal comes with many forceful associations, including persistence, strength, and determination. It has a solid shape that gives structure and, as such, people ruled by the metal element are sometimes inflexible and stubborn.

In Chinese culture, the metal element is symbolized by a white tiger. It governs the Chinese zodiac signs Monkey, Rooster, and Dog.

The Celtic Zodiac

Practiced by the ancient Irish and derived from the
Druids' deep association with nature, Celtic tree astrology
divides the year into thirteen lunar months. A tree, a
sacred symbol, is assigned to each month.

Trees, as vessels of infinite wisdom, have individual
qualities that are reflected in human personalities.
Their roots represent the past, their trunks represent
the present, and the branches symbolize both the
future and the afterlife.

The tree signs of the Celtic zodiac are Birch,
Rowan, Ash, Alder, Willow, Hawthorn, Oak,
Holly, Hazel, Vine, Ivy, Reed, and Elder.

The Egyptian Zodiac

One of the oldest zodiac systems, the Egyptian zodiac is based on the mythology of ancient Egyptian gods and is determined by birth date. The zodiac includes twelve signs: The Nile, Amon-Ra, Mut, Geb, Osiris, Isis, Thoth, Horus, Anubis, Seth, Bastet, and Sekhmet.

Egyptian astrologers believe that your life's path is predetermined by the sign you are born under, and your personal characteristics can be attributed to the deity of that sign.

The Mayan Zodiac

The ancient Mayans believed that the will of the gods could be read in the sky. They recorded the movements of the stars, planets, and Moon, which formed the basis of a complex calendar system.

The Mayan Haab system is based on a calendar with eighteen months and five nameless days, with nineteen corresponding signs. According to Mayan tradition, an individual's core sign is determined by their birth month and date. Unlike other systems, the Mayans did not attribute specific characteristics to the signs.

The Native American Zodiac

The Medicine Wheel, sometimes known as the Sacred Hoop, has been used by generations of Native Americans to represent all of the knowledge in the universe. Placing great importance on the seasons, the wheel represents a complete year and embodies four directions—east, south, west, and north, symbolizing the cycles of life.

Within the wheel, the year is split into four sections, or "clans." Each clan is further divided into sections represented by an animal totem: Goose, Otter, Wolf, Hawk, Beaver, Deer, Woodpecker, Salmon, Bear, Raven, Snake, and Owl.

The Vedic Zodiac

Vedic astrology is also known as Indian astrology, Hindu astrology, or Jyotisha, which means "the science of light." The zodiac wheel is made up of twelve zodiac signs plus twenty-seven nakshatras, which are constellations based on the movement of the Moon. Each nakshatra has its own ruling deity, which plays a role in defining the characteristics of an individual.

Vedic astrology seeks to provide guidance for the journey of life, while also taking into account the influence of free will on destiny. Vedic horoscopes are traditionally used to help determine the best course of action to achieve spiritual growth.

The Sun

The Sun, giver of all life, is a symbol of the conscious mind. It represents the creative life force and our will to live. Just as the planets revolve around the Sun, the Sun shapes the meaning of the astrological signs.

The Moon

The eight phases of the Moon are incredibly impactful in astrological terms. The Moon cycle is similar to that of a seed: growing, blossoming, and dying.

The Moon, in its various forms, signifies intuition, wisdom, birth, death, and reincarnation. The owl, with its links to the night and mysterious knowledge, acts as a symbol of this unearthly power.

The Planets

Before the age of telescopes, astrologers based their learnings on the seven celestial bodies that could be seen with the naked eye. These were the Moon, the Sun, Mercury, Venus, Mars, Jupiter, and Saturn.

To ancient astrologers, the planets represented the will of the gods. Each planet has different, distinctive qualities that are manifested in the signs of the zodiac.

The Astrologer

An expert in the language of the stars, the
astrologer observes and interprets the influence
of celestial bodies on human destiny.

Using birth charts, astrologers are able to read into the
past, present, and future, creating a framework that
enables us to understand more about our lives and
discover the secrets of our deepest selves.

Stargazing

It is possible to spot zodiac constellations with the naked eye—just like astrologers did 2,000 years ago. As the Sun's path lies within these groups of stars, you can look for them along the path that the Sun follows during the day. The darker and clearer the night sky, the better chance there is of identifying specific constellations.